ZEN-ON SINFONIETTA SERIES

Shin-ichiro IKEBE

VIVACIOUS LINES
for the Strings

池辺晋一郎

ヴィヴェイシャス・ラインズ
弦楽のために

zen-on music

VIVACIOUS LINES
for the Strings

Commissioned by "Yokohama Virtuoso"

First Performance: September 5th, 2009
Yokohama Minato Mirai Hall (Small Hall)

The title of this work "Vivacious Lines" parallels my previous work "Elegiac Lines" (1982, published by Zen-On Music Co., Ltd.)

Shin-ichiro IKEBE

《ヴィヴェイシャス・ラインズ》 弦楽オーケストラのために

委嘱：ヴィルトゥオーゾ横浜
初演：2009年9月5日　横浜みなとみらいホール（小ホール）
　　　ヴィルトゥオーゾ横浜
演奏時間：約12分

《ヴィヴェイシャス・ラインズ》（vivacious＝陽気な）は、1982年の作品《エレジアック・ラインズ》（elegiac＝哀しみの）（全音楽譜出版社刊）に対応するものである。

池辺晋一郎

INSTRUMENTATION

Violins I
Violins II
Violas
Violoncellos
Double Basses

Duration: approximately 12 minutes

Material is available on hire.

ZEN-ON MUSIC, Tokyo

VIVACIOUS LINES
for the Strings

Shin-ichiro IKEBE
(2009)

©2016 by Zen-On Music Co., Ltd.

20

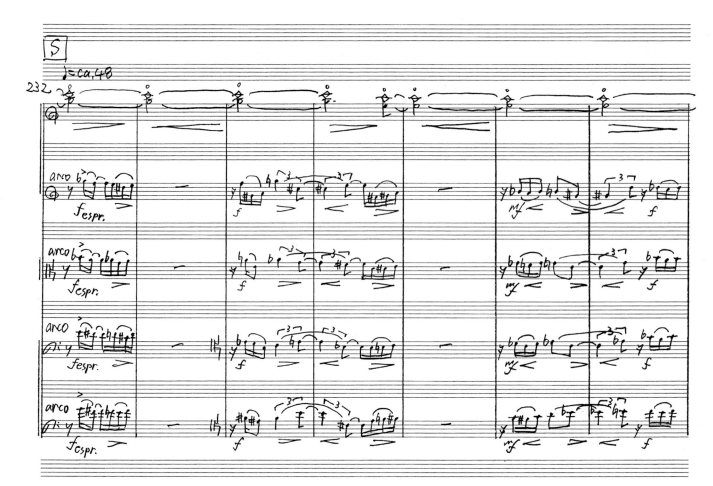

25

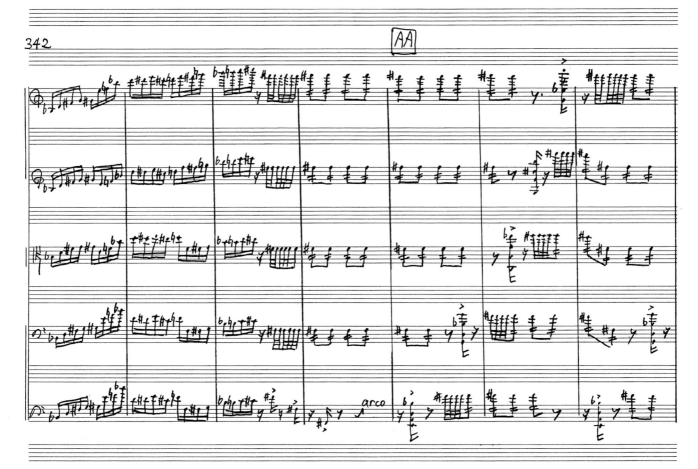

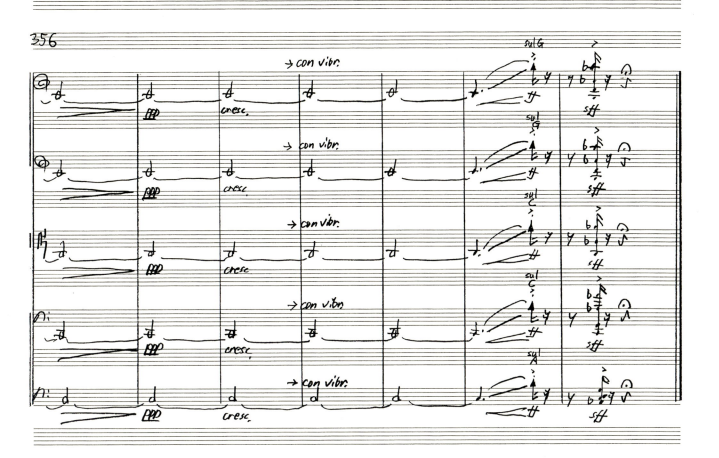

(16th Aug., 2009 Sapporo)

ヴィヴェイシャス・ラインズ	●
作曲	池辺晋一郎
第1版第1刷発行	2016年9月15日
発行	株式会社全音楽譜出版社
	東京都新宿区上落合2丁目13番3号 〒161-0034
	TEL・営業部 03・3227-6270
	出版部 03・3227-6280
	URL http://www.zen-on.co.jp/
	ISBN978-4-11-900029-8

複写・複製・転載等厳禁　Printed in Japan

16090135

ISBN978-4-11-900029-8

C3073 ¥1800E

定価[本体1,800円+税]

定価[本体1,800円+税]